Little Pebble™

Healthy Me

WITHDRAWN

I EAT WELL

by Martha E. H. Rustad

CAPSTONE PRESS
a capstone imprint

Little Pebble is published by Capstone Press,
1710 Roe Crest Drive, North Mankato, Minnesota 56003
www.mycapstone.com

Library of Congress Cataloging-in-Publication Data
Names: Rustad, Martha E. H. (Martha Elizabeth Hillman), 1975- author.
Title: I eat well / by Martha E.H. Rustad.
Description: : North Mankato, Minnesota : Capstone Press, [2017]
 Series: Little pebble. Healthy me | Includes bibliographical references and index.
Identifiers: LCCN 2016032850
ISBN 9781515739838 (library binding)
ISBN 9781515739876 (paperback)
ISBN 9781515739999 (eBook PDF)
Subjects: LCSH: Nutrition—Juvenile literature. | Health—Juvenile literature.
Classification: LCC RA784 .R87 2017 | DDC 613.2—dc23
LC record available at https://lccn.loc.gov/2016032850

Editorial Credits
Shelly Lyons, editor; Juliette Peters, designer;
Jo Miller, media researcher; Tori Abraham, production specialist

Photo Credits
Images by Capstone Studio: Karon Dubke
Photo styling: Sarah Schuette and Marcy Morin

Printed and bound in China.
007885

Table of Contents

Morning

I am a busy kid!

My body needs fuel.

I eat well.

I eat breakfast.

Yogurt has protein.

It fills me up.

Dad adds nuts.

I add berries.

Snack time!

I peel a banana.

Fruit has vitamins.

They help my body grow.

Afternoon

Lunch bell!

We eat pasta.

We drink milk.

Green salad has minerals.

I eat a snack after school.
Carrots fill me up.

Soccer!

I drink lots of water.

Water keeps me cool.

Evening

Let's cook supper!

I cut a tomato with Mom.

My brother shreds cheese.

We eat chicken wraps.

Mmm!

I love sweets.

But dessert is a rare treat.

Tasty!

Good food helps
my body grow.
Eating well means
a healthy me!

21

Glossary

dessert—a sweet food eaten at the end of a meal

mineral—a substance the body needs; iron and calcium are minerals.

protein—something in food the body uses to build and repair itself; meat, nuts, and beans are high in protein.

rare—not often seen, found, or happening

vitamin—tiny bits inside food that the body needs; Vitamin D helps bones; Vitamin A helps eyes.

yogurt—a thick food made from milk

Read More

Bodden, Valerie. *Eating Healthy.* Healthy Plates. Mankato, Minn.: Creative Education, 2015.

Boothroyd, Jennifer. *What's on My Plate?* Healthy Eating. Minneapolis: Lerner, 2016.

Sjonger, Rebecca. *Healthy Habits for a Lifetime: How to Choose Foods Your Body Will Use.* New York: Crabtree, 2016.

Internet Sites

FactHound offers a safe, fun way to find Internet sites related to this book. All of the sites on FactHound have been researched by our staff.

Here's all you do:
Visit *www.facthound.com*
Type in this code: 9781515739838

Check out projects, games and lots more at
www.capstonekids.com

Critical Thinking Using the Common Core

1. What does yogurt contain?
   (Key Ideas and Details)

2. Why is it important to drink water?
   (Integration of Knowledge and Ideas)

3. Greens contain minerals. What is a mineral?
   (Craft and Structure)

Index